Travel Journal
Washington DC

VPJournals

Copyright © 2015 VPJournals

All rights reserved.

ISBN-13: 978-1518844744
ISBN-10: 151884474X

Contact Details

Name: _____

Email address: _____

Tel: _____

Address: _____

_____

Important Medical Information

Blood type: _____

Medication: _____

CONTENTS

Hi, I hope you enjoy this journal. It is packed with cool stuff and recommendations for you trip to Washington DC, and has plenty of space to record details of your trip.

What's Inside	Page
Before you go to Washington DC	
Great places to visit in Washington DC	6-7
Cool places to visit in Washington DC with kids	8-9
Good places to eat	10-11
Research Washington DC	12-13
Postcard & Packing List	14-19
Washington DC facts	21-22
Helpful hints	23-26
Clothes and shoe sizing charts, to help you get the right sizes while there	
Washington DC Trip Diary	27-111
21 day trip diary to record details of your trip	
Reflect on you Trip	
Summary of your trip	113-121
People you met	123-125
Useful Resources	127-136
Size conversion charts	129-132
Common Translations	133-134
Notes	135-136

Have fun in Washington DC

Great Places to visit in Washington DC

National Gallery of Art	✓
Lincoln Memorial and Reflecting Pool	
Basilica of the National Shrine of the Immaculate Conception	
Library of Congress	
Franklin Delano Roosevelt Memorial	
United States Holocaust Memorial Museum	
Korean War Veterans Memorial	
Hillwood Museum & Gardens	
Newseum	
Vietnam Veterans Memorial	
National Mall	

National Portrait Gallery	
Jefferson Memorial	
National World War II Memorial	
Smithsonian National Air and Space Museum	
Washington National Cathedral	
John F. Kennedy Center for the Performing Arts	
The Phillips Collection	
Smithsonian Institution Building	
Smithsonian American Art Museum	
Smithsonian National Museum of Natural History	
Ford's Theatre	
The White House	

Cool Places to visit in Washington DC with Kids

National Zoo	✓
National Museum of Natural History	
National Air & Space Museum	
National Children's Museum	
Discovery Theater	
National Museum of American History	
Bureau of Engraving & Printing	
Washington Monument	
Lincoln Memorial and Reflecting Pool	
US Holocaust Memorial Museum	
National Portrait Gallery	

Glen Echo Park	
Six Flags America	
Watch a game (Reskins, DC United Soccer)	
Imagination Stage	
Wolf Trap National Park	
Rock Creek Nature Center	
Reston Zoo	
The White House	
International Spy Museum	
Library of Congress	
Interactive Museum of News: The Newseum	
Bealeton Flying Circus Airshow	
Cabin John Regional Park	

Good Places to Eat in Washington DC

Barmini	✓
Keren Coffee Shop	
Baked and Wired	
Zaytinya	
Rasika	
Bub and Pop's	
Rose's Luxury	
Corduroy	
H &pizza	
Marcel's	
Pho Viet	
The Capital Grille	

Le Diplomate	
Red Hen	
Blue Duck Tavern	
Rasika West End	
Bar Dupont	
JoJo Restaurant and Bar	
Fogo de Chao	
Old Ebbitt Grill	
Joe's Seafood, Prime Steak and Stone Crab	
Founding Farmers	
Reseach and add more here	

Best Websites to Research Further

Do some more research on the internet to plan your trip:

www.washington.org
www.dc.gov/page/visitors-resource-center
www.placesinwashingtondc.com
www.thedistrict.com
www.nps.gov/nr/travel/wash/sitelist.htm
www.wikipedia.org/wiki/Washington,_D.C.
www.lonelyplanet.com/usa/washington-dc
www.wikitravel.org/en/Washington,_D.C.
www.washingtonpost.com/goingoutguide/
www.trolleytours.com/washington-dc/

More places I want to visit on our trip

1. _____
2. _____
3. _____
4. _____
5. _____
6. _____
7. _____
8. _____
9. _____
10. _____
11. _____
12. _____
13. _____
14. _____
15. _____

Postcard List

Name:
Address:

Name:
Address:

Name:
Address:

Name:

Address:

Name:

Address:

Name:

Address:

Name:

Address:

Name:

Address:

Name:

Address:

Name:

Address:

Name:

Address:

Name:

Address:

Name:

Address:

Name:

Address:

Packing List

✓	This Journal
	Tickets
	Passport
	Money
	Chargers
	Batteries
	Book to read
	Camera
	Tablet
	Sun glasses
	Sun cream

	Toiletries
	Water
	Watch
	Snacks
	Umbrella
	Towel
	Guide book
	Kindle
	Jacket
	Medication
	Add more below

Washington DC Facts

- Washington takes its name from the first president of the United States, George Washington. The "Columbia" in "District of Columbia" stands for Christopher Columbus

- The people who live in Washington, DC are called Washingtonians

- When the Washington Monument opened to the public in 1888, it was the tallest structure in the world until the Eiffel Tower in Paris opened in 1889

- The Library of Congress is the biggest library in the United States. It has 535 miles of bookshelves

- Most of Washington DC's attractions are free

- The National Mall is a national park and the central point of most sightseeing visits in downtown Washington D.C.

- The White House has a total of 35 bathrooms

- The International Spy Museum is the only public museum in America that is all about spies. Learn first-hand how to go undercover as a super spy

- There are about 2,000 animals from 400 different species at the National Zoo

- You can play reporter for a day or go behind the camera and see if you have what it takes to be a photographer at the NBC News Interactive Newsroom at the Newseum

- You can come face to face with all 44 Presidents or pose with your favorite rock star or actress at Madame Tussauds Washington D.C.

- You can watch money being printed when you check out a tour of the Bureau of Engraving and Printing

- Washington, DC is not a city or state, nor is it part of any other state. It is a unique "federal district," created specifically to be the seat of government.

- George Washington never lived in DC. The White House was actually completed a year after he died. Second President, John Adams, was the first to live there

Clothes & Shoe Sizes

Children's Shoe Sizes

UK	EUROPE	US	Japan
4	20	4½ or 5	12 ½
4 ½	21	5 or 5½	13
5	21 or 22	5½ or 6	13 ½
5 ½	22	6	13½ or 14
6	23	6½ or 7	14 or 14½
6 ½	23 or 24	7 ½	14½ or 15
7	24	7½ or 8	15
7 ½	25	8 or 9	15 ½
8	25 or 26	8½ or 9	16
8 ½	26	9½	16 ½
9	27	9½ or 10	16 ½ or 17
10	28	10½ or 11	17 ½
10½ or 11	29	11½ or 12	18
11 ½	30	12½	18 or 18 ½
12	31	13	19 or 19 ½
12 ½	31	13 or 13½	19 ½ or 20
13	32	1	20
13 ½	32 ½	1 ½	20 ½
1	33	1½ or 2	21
2	34	2½ or 3	22

Children's Clothing Sizes

UK	EUROPE	US	Australia
12m	80cm	12-18m	12m
18m	80-86cm	18-24m	18m
24m	86-92cm	23-24m	2
2-3	92-98cm	2T	3
3-4	98-104cm	4T	4
3-5	104-110cm	5	5
5-6	110-116cm	6	6
6-7	116-122cm	6X-7	7
7-8	122-128cm	7 to 8	8
8-9	128-134cm	9 to 10	9
9-10	134-140cm	10	10
10-11	140-146cm	11	11
11-12	146-152cm	14	12

Women's Shoe Sizes

UK	EUROPE	US	Japan
3	35 ½	5	22 ½
3 ½	36	5 ½	23
4	37	6	23
4 ½	37 ½	6 ½	23 ½
5	38	7	24
5 ½	39	7 ½	24
6	39 ½	8	24 ½
6 ½	40	8 ½	25
7	41	9 ½	25 ½
7 ½	41 ½	10	26
8	42	10 ½	26 ½

Women's Clothes Sizes

UK	US	Japan	France / Spain	Germany	Washington DC	Australia
6/8	6	7-9	36	34	40	8
10	8	9-11	38	36	42	10
12	10	11-13	40	38	44	12
14	12	13-15	42	39	46	14
16	14	15-17	44	40	48	16
18	16	17-19	46	42	50	18
20	18	19-21	48	44	52	20

Men's Shoe Sizes

UK	EUROPE	US	Japan
6	38 ½	6 ½	24 ½
6 ½	39	7	25
7	40	7 ½	25 ½
7 ½	41	8	26
8	42	8 ½	27 ½
8 ½	43	9	27 ½
9	43 ½	9 ½	28
9 ½	44	10	28 ½
10	44	10 ½	28 ½
10 ½	44 ½	11	29
11	45	12	29 ½

Men's Suit / Coat / Sweater Sizes

UK / US / Aus	EU / Japan	General
32	42	Small
34	44	Small
36	46	Small
38	48	Medium
40	50	Large
42	52	Large
44	54	Extra Large
46	56	Extra Large

Men's Pants / Trouser Sizes (Waist)

UK / US	Europe
32	81 cm
34	86 cm
36	91 cm
38	97 cm
40	102 cm
42	107 cm

We have included another copy of this at the back of the book, so you can find it quickly again when you are in Washington DC

Washington DC Trip Diary

Write a daily diary during your trip

Day 1

Date: _____   **Weather:** _____

Day 2

Date: _____   **Weather:** _____

Day 3

Date: **Weather:**

Day 4

Date: _____   **Weather:** _____

Day 5

Tip! Send your postcards

Date: **Weather:**

Day 6

Date: _____   **Weather:** _____

Day 7

Date: _____   **Weather:** _____

Day 8

Date: _____   **Weather:** _____

Day 9

Date: **Weather:**

Day 10

Date: _____   **Weather:** _____

Day 11

Date: _____   **Weather:** _____

Day 12

Date: **Weather:**

Day 13

Date: _____ Weather: _____

Day 14

Date: **Weather:**

Day 15

Date: _____   Weather: _____

Day 16

Date: _____   **Weather:** _____

Day 17

Date: **Weather:**

Day 18

Date: _____   Weather: _____

Day 19

Date: _____ Weather: _____

Day 20

Date: **Weather:**

Day 21

Date: **Weather:**

Memories of your Trip

Things I will remember from the trip

Favorite Places visited on the Trip

People I Met

Name:
Address:
Tel:
email:

Name:
Address:
Tel:
email:

Name:
Address:
Tel:
email:

Name:
Address:
Tel:
email:

Name:
Address:
Tel:
email:

Name:
Address:
Tel:
email:

Name:
Address:
Tel:
email:

Name:	
Address:	
Tel:	
email:	

Name:	
Address:	
Tel:	
email:	

Name:	
Address:	
Tel:	
email:	

Name:	
Address:	
Tel:	
email:	

We hope you enjoyed your trip to Washington DC

Please leave us a review if you found this Journal useful

Check out our useful resources on the next few pages

Clothes & Shoe Sizes

Children's Shoe Sizes

UK	EUROPE	US	Japan
4	20	4½ or 5	12 ½
4 ½	21	5 or 5½	13
5	21 or 22	5½ or 6	13 ½
5 ½	22	6	13½ or 14
6	23	6½ or 7	14 or 14½
6 ½	23 or 24	7 ½	14½ or 15
7	24	7½ or 8	15
7 ½	25	8 or 9	15 ½
8	25 or 26	8½ or 9	16
8 ½	26	9½	16 ½
9	27	9½ or 10	16 ½ or 17
10	28	10½ or 11	17 ½
10½ or 11	29	11½ or 12	18
11 ½	30	12½	18 or 18 ½
12	31	13	19 or 19 ½
12 ½	31	13 or 13½	19 ½ or 20
13	32	1	20
13 ½	32 ½	1 ½	20 ½
1	33	1½ or 2	21
2	34	2½ or 3	22

Children's Clothing Sizes

UK	EUROPE	US	Australia
12m	80cm	12-18m	12m
18m	80-86cm	18-24m	18m
24m	86-92cm	23-24m	2
2-3	92-98cm	2T	3
3-4	98-104cm	4T	4
3-5	104-110cm	5	5
5-6	110-116cm	6	6
6-7	116-122cm	6X-7	7
7-8	122-128cm	7 to 8	8
8-9	128-134cm	9 to 10	9
9-10	134-140cm	10	10
10-11	140-146cm	11	11
11-12	146-152cm	14	12

Women's Shoe Sizes

UK	EUROPE	US	Japan
3	35 ½	5	22 ½
3 ½	36	5 ½	23
4	37	6	23
4 ½	37 ½	6 ½	23 ½
5	38	7	24
5 ½	39	7 ½	24
6	39 ½	8	24 ½
6 ½	40	8 ½	25
7	41	9 ½	25 ½
7 ½	41 ½	10	26
8	42	10 ½	26 ½

Women's Clothes Sizes

UK	US	Japan	France / Spain	Germany	Washington DC	Australia
6/8	6	7-9	36	34	40	8
10	8	9-11	38	36	42	10
12	10	11-13	40	38	44	12
14	12	13-15	42	39	46	14
16	14	15-17	44	40	48	16
18	16	17-19	46	42	50	18
20	18	19-21	48	44	52	20

Men's Shoe Sizes

UK	EUROPE	US	Japan
6	38 ½	6 ½	24 ½
6 ½	39	7	25
7	40	7 ½	25 ½
7 ½	41	8	26
8	42	8 ½	27 ½
8 ½	43	9	27 ½
9	43 ½	9 ½	28
9 ½	44	10	28 ½
10	44	10 ½	28 ½
10 ½	44 ½	11	29
11	45	12	29 ½

Men's Suit / Coat / Sweater Sizes

UK / US / Aus	EU / Japan	General
32	42	Small
34	44	Small
36	46	Small
38	48	Medium
40	50	Large
42	52	Large
44	54	Extra Large
46	56	Extra Large

Men's Pants / Trouser Sizes (Waist)

UK / US	Europe
32	81 cm
34	86 cm
36	91 cm
38	97 cm
40	102 cm
42	107 cm

Common Translations

English	French	Spanish	Italian
Hello	Bonjour	Hola	Ciao
Goodbye	Au revoir	Adiós	Arrivederci
Yes	Oui	Sí	Si
No	Non	No	No
Please	S'il-vous-plaît	Por favor	Per favore
Thank you	Merci	Gracias	Grazie
Excuse me	Excusez-moi	Perdón	Mi scusi
How much	Combien	Cuánto	Quanto
My name is	Mon nom est	Mi nombre es	Io mi chiamo
Where is	Où est	Dónde está	Dov'è
The bank	La banque	El banco	La banca
The toilet	Les toilettes	El baño	Il bagno

German	Japanese	Mandarin	Hindi
Hallo	Kon'nichiwa	Ni hao	Namaste
Auf Wiedersehen	Sayonara	Zaijian	Alavida
Ja	Hai	Shi de	Ham
Nein	Ie	Meiyou	Nahim
Bitte	Onegaishimasu	Qing	Krpaya
Vielen Dank	Arigato	Xiexie	Dhan'yavada
Entschuldigung	Sumimasen	Duoshao	Mujhe mapha karem
Wie viel	Ikura	Wo de mingzi shi	Kitana
Mein Name ist	Watashinonamaeha	Nali	Mera nama hai
Wo ist	Doko ni aru	Yinhang	Kaham hai
Die Bank	Ginko	Yinhang	Bainka
Die Toilette	Toire	Cesuo	Saucalaya

Notes:

84036096R00077

Made in the USA
Lexington, KY
18 March 2018